Eyes of Wonder

Rebecca,
Thank you for bringing hope and inspiration to others by sharing your stories. Keep shining!
Shauna Gabriel

Eyes of Wonder

How to Recapture Your Childlike Spirit

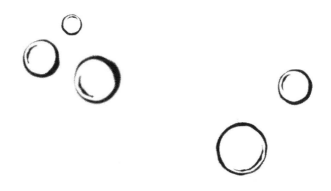

Laurie Gabriel

Copyright © 2020 Laurie Gabriel

All rights reserved. Photographs used herein are owned by the author. No portion of this book may be reproduced, stored in a retrieval system, or transmitted in any form or by any means—electronic, mechanical, photocopy, recording, scanning, or other—except for brief quotations in critical reviews or articles, without the prior written permission of the author.

Published in the United States.

Laurie Gabriel, 1962–
TITLE: Eyes of Wonder: How to Recapture Your Childlike Spirit | Laurie Gabriel.
DESCRIPTION: First edition, 2020.
KEYWORDS: Childlike spirit. | Imagination and creativity. | Presence and better focus. | Self-image. | Relationships and friendships.
ISBN-13: 979-8683834265

Library of Congress Control Number: 2020916864

Interior design by Cheri Gillard
Cover photograph by Eric Weber

TABLE OF CONTENTS

Introduction		i
Chapter 1	Focus	1
Chapter 2	Be Curious	15
Chapter 3	Use Your Imagination	26
Chapter 4	Be Creative	40
Chapter 5	Play	51
Chapter 6	Appreciate Nature	60
Chapter 7	See Everyone as a Friend	70
Chapter 8	Share	84
Chapter 9	Don't Judge by Appearance	94
Chapter 10	Show Your Feelings	104
Supplemental Material		115

INTRODUCTION

I've spent most of my dual career in sort of a middle ground between pre-teens and the elderly. I've learned something from both groups.

From my middle-school students, I've learned that sixth grade is just about the time when kids seem to let go of all kinds of childhood traits that would actually benefit them as adults: creativity, healthy self-esteem, compassion, imagination, and a sense of oneness with the universe.

From the senior populations that I frequently entertain, I've learned that we will likely regret letting go of those childhood qualities and will spend a lot of time trying to get them back.

I'm not saying we all had a perfect childhood. Some of us, including myself, had difficulties we'd rather forget. I'm not necessarily referring to revisiting specific events from our past; rather, I'm talking about getting in touch with the nature we had as children. We were more forgiving, more open, more curious, and more present.

What if we could hold on to our childlike sense of wonder and awe, along with our playful inhibitions and a clear sense of our place in humanity, throughout our lives? I'm not sure why we lose those characteristics so readily or why we encourage others to do the same, but perhaps if we held onto those qualities it would bring a change for the better.

We can't change all at once. We are firmly embedded in our routines and customs. But five minutes a day spent reminding ourselves of the freedom and innocence of childhood could set us on a new course—one that would benefit us all.

I've added some exercises to the end of each chapter. These aren't meant to be considered all at once; that would be overwhelming. They are simply meant to be tried one at a time in small doses. Some require just five minutes, some are a focus to carry through a single day, and others are larger commitments. Some are there to spark happiness or provide a break from the boredom of routine, and others have a broad global connotation. Pick and choose those that resonate with you or those you think you need the most. If one doesn't work for you, try another. The process unfolds best if you create a system that allows you to routinely work through the checklist, perhaps committing to one item per day or per week and keeping track of your progress.

I started this project because these were lessons I needed to learn myself. I am still learning. It is my hope that this book helps you rediscover all those positive traits you may have lost along the way and rekindle a joyful connection with your surrounding world and with your own inner spirit.

The author at age four

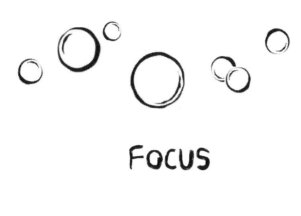

Focus

1

DO YOU REMEMBER when you could become completely focused on some random object and lose all track of time? Maybe it was water swirling down the drain, or a bug crawling on the sidewalk, or the moon. I remember being fascinated with the patterns in the fabric of my mother's dresses. Did you have a toy that you played with for hours? It might have been a dollhouse, a train set, a model airplane, or a toy piano. Somehow you could block out everything else that was happening in the world and put all your attention on that object.

We often tell kids they are not focusing, but

what we really mean is that they are not focusing on the things we have deemed important. As we get older, we are taught to put our attention on things we equate with progress. If an activity is not inching us closer to that dream job in the future, we label it as not worthwhile. Once we are caught up in the whirlwind of "productivity," we start to yearn for an escape, sometimes even spending our hard-earned money on seminars that teach us how we can be more present and focused on the things that really matter.

What if we never left that space in the first place? Yes, in order to have homes, cars, food, and clothing, we need to do things that are of value to the world and can therefore earn us a paycheck, but somewhere there is a balance.

Society rewards multitasking and overachievement, but there is a benefit to letting your brain tune out all the noise and distraction of daily life, including the nagging voices that live inside our own heads. Those voices weren't there when we were young children. You wouldn't find a toddler bemoaning some mistake from the previous day or worrying about all she has to do tomorrow. When did those voices first creep in, and how do we make them go away?

There is an easy, no-cost way to escape into presence at any time and place, and that is the practice of noticing things. Just like when we were children playing "I Spy with My Little Eye," we can decide to look at things that we ordinarily take for granted. Simply stop what you are doing, set a timer for five minutes, and choose something to notice: red things, tiny things, square things, etc. You will find that you can quickly take yourself into a state of calm. This technique can be effective against pain, depression, boredom, anger, nervousness, and other feelings we might wish to avoid, even if it is only temporary.

I conducted my own little study with a group of thirty friends. We chose a different focus item each day, and by the end of the month-long study, my friends reported feeling happier and more relaxed. We also felt we had increased our creativity and improved our concentration.

Another benefit was that we became aware of beautiful things we previously would have overlooked, like ice crystals on a branch, tail lights reflecting on wet pavement, sunlight gleaming through a transparent leaf, or interesting door designs. We found ourselves doing the method throughout the day instead of just the five-minute minimum, and each day it became more automatic.

I had a calendar hanging in my house that featured beautiful images painted by Thomas Kinkade. I'd walked by each of those pages every day for a month and thought I'd paid attention to it. When I finally looked at it with true focus, I found all kinds of lovely details I'd never seen: a horse and carriage far off in the distance, a rainbow-colored waterfall, a family of rabbits, etc. I was amazed to discover how many pretty details I'd overlooked.

I have tried the practice of hyperfocus with my teenaged cello students at their private lessons. If I have a student who is particularly squirmy or is starting to lose focus, I pause the lesson and ask her to look around the room for a certain thing, like circles or soft things. Once the student has done that for about a minute, she is able to get back to the lesson and stay focused for a good while.

Another thing we rarely consider is the

craftsmanship that went into every human-made object we see. If you sit for a minute and look at every item that is in your view, you can become overwhelmed thinking about the number of humans that were involved in the conception, creation, and delivery of that item. From any spot in my house, I can see dozens of items to appreciate—furniture, lighting fixtures, electronics, books, carpeting, a gas fireplace, paintings, pots for plants—all here for my enjoyment because of something strangers invented or made. It can make me feel quite wealthy thinking of the thousands of people involved in the existence of just the things in one small area of my house.

Take my skirt, for example. Someone had to come up with the design, another had to make the textiles, another had to sew the pieces together, another had to package it, and another had to deliver it to the store. This doesn't even take into account the people who built the factory where the skirt was made and all the components of metal and glass and wood that went into building that factory, or the people who made the truck that transported it, or the people who built the roads between the factory and the store, or the people who work at the store. The amount of people directly or indirectly involved in me having this skirt are seemingly endless.

If you really want to feel global, go through your closet and look at the tags. I counted thirty-four different countries on my clothing labels. Each morning when I get dressed, I like to take special notice of the design and construction of every garment. It gives me a feeling of gratitude for human craftsmanship.

Hyperfocusing can also be done with sound. We don't often take time to listen to all the sounds we can hear at one time. As I sit on my porch writing this, I simultaneously hear wind rustling through the trees, a dog barking, water in my fountain, my neighbor opening his screen door, cars, birds, an airplane, and some kids playing in the distance. These are not sounds I typically notice unless I'm intently focused on hearing them. We might find some of these sounds annoying, but when we take ten minutes to focus on nothing but sound, a certain calm can arise, and we forget about the problems that were occupying our thoughts.

Listening for distinct, separate sounds has another benefit: it can improve our hearing and make us less likely to need a hearing aid later in life. Studies, such as one performed at the University of Kansas by Dr. Brenda Hanna-Pladdy, have shown that musicians and music conductors are much better than the average person at tuning out sounds they don't want to hear in order to focus on what they do want to hear. This is because they have spent their lives listening for specific things in the groups in which they play. As a conductor, I'm able to train my ear to listen for just the violas or just the clarinet amidst all the other instrumental sounds. You can do this yourself with a recording. Play a piece of orchestral music and listen through, concentrating on one specific instrument. You'll notice harmonies you may never have noticed, because we normally put our focus on the main melody. Try it with a pop song and listen just for the bass or the drums. You can even pretend you're playing the instrument if no one's looking.

Another thing you can try is assigning yourself a "sound of the day." Take note each time you hear a bird chirping, water running, a light switch clicking, or a certain word being spoken. It can bring a sense of anticipation and alertness to an otherwise routine day. Another thing I like to do is pay attention to sound effects when I'm watching a movie. What items did the Foley artist use to create each effect? How did the composer use music to sway the emotions of the audience?

Once you've mastered your focus on visual and aural stimuli, move on to your other senses. How often do we take time to pay attention to our food? Children do. Babies swish food all over their mouths, feeling the texture with their tongues. What they are really doing is being present about eating, which is known to be beneficial. It helps us appreciate what's on our plates and keeps us from gorging. Instead of telling our kids to hurry and finish, perhaps we could find a way to give them more time to enjoy their meals. We need that reminder as adults, too. I often find myself gulping my food straight from the container at the kitchen counter. It's much more pleasurable when I take time to relish the taste and texture of each bite.

The same is true for smells. How often do we focus on the aroma of our food, the scent of the rain, our children's freshly-washed hair, a burning candle, or a flower we pass on the way to work? Yes, you may come across some smells you wish weren't there, but there is a calm center that comes with using this sense, and some of our most powerful memories are stored within it.

Don't forget the sense of touch. We often tune out our sensitivity to what is touching our skin. We select clothing based on the look and not necessarily the comfort of the fabric. We take for granted the pleasantness of a soft sheet, a fluffy pillow, or bare feet on lush grass. Spend a day being alert to the feel of textiles, surfaces, and even the brush of wind on your skin. Bring the focus even closer by noticing specifically what your hands are touching or by paying attention to what's underneath your feet.

Awareness of our senses can bring immediate calm and can also help us craft environments that give us maximum enjoyment. With a little bit of practice, it's easy to slip in and out of this peaceful, meditative state just as a child does.

My son intently focusing on his toy

☑ Try This

☐ Pick a letter and look for words that begin with it. You can do this for five minutes or make it an all-day challenge. What's the longest word you saw?

☐ Choose a letter and listen for words that start with that letter for a determined length of time. What's the most interesting word you heard?

☐ Use the "Focus List" in the supplemental materials at the end of this book to choose a focus item of the day. Add your own ideas to the list. Look for that item whenever you're bored, when you need to refocus, or any time your mind starts to fill with unwanted thoughts.

☐ Count how many times you see a certain object (signs, neckties, water bottles, eyeglasses, etc.) during a designated time period. Have a contest with someone else to see who can find the most.

☐ Spend a day noticing the smallest things in view: bugs, crumbs, lint, etc. Or look for the farthest things you can see in the distance.

☐ Stare at a calendar picture, painting, illustration, piece of printed fabric, elaborate rug, ornate furnishing, or wallpaper pattern for five minutes. Search for details that might previously have gone unnoticed.

☐ When in a crowded place (or while watching TV), focus on one specific human characteristic: mouths, ears, eyes, eyebrows, hairstyles, hands, etc.

☐ Look at an item and consider all the people who may have been involved in its creation.

☐ Look for design. Notice details in building facades, lighting fixtures, automobiles, book covers, or decor.

☐ Go through your closet and notice where each item was made. How many different countries did you find?

☐ Look for a "mini story." Watch a bug cross the sidewalk, two birds chirping back and forth, or a person walking through the airport. Stick with it for at least one minute.

☐ Take one minute to listen for all the different sounds you can hear. How many did you find?

☐ Spend a day noticing one particular sound: birds singing, children laughing, doors opening, silverware clanking, music, the wind, etc.

☐ Watch a movie or TV show and think about what went into the sound effects and music in the background.

☐ Listen to live or recorded music and focus on one particular instrument. Pretend you are the person playing that instrument.

☐ Listen to someone else speak for a full minute without saying anything. Focus on the tone of the voice and on the emotion behind what the person is saying.

☐ Do a blind "taste test" with friends or family. Try different wines, sodas, or foods. Focus on distinguishing different tastes.

FOCUS

☐ Spend a day savoring every bite of food you eat.

☐ Spend a day noticing the feel of different textures against your skin. Which are the most pleasurable? How can you eliminate or improve the less pleasurable ones? Consider donating clothing or shoes that aren't comfortable.

☐ Spend a day noticing your hands and all the different things they do, or pay attention to all the different surfaces that pass underneath your feet.

Be Curious

2

ANYONE WHO HAS raised a child is familiar with that stage when the child asks, "Why?" in response to just about everything. Why is the sky blue? Why do people get old? Why can't we go out in the cold without a coat?

It's natural and appropriate for children to question things, yet in our exasperation we sometimes ask them to be quiet and just accept that sometimes there are no answers. However, a lack of answers to certain questions does not mean we should give up asking. I'm sure Thomas Edison, Albert Einstein, and Elon Musk would agree.

I have worked in academic settings where asking questions was discouraged. The establishment seemed more interested in students memorizing someone else's answers than in having them come up with their own. This has led to a shortage of creative problem-solvers in the workplace.

Many of us may feel we don't have time to explore our curiosity, but if we could take the time to allow just a little space for learning new things, we would immediately feel the benefits. Our brains have evolved to release positive chemicals, such as serotonin and dopamine, when we explore new things.

Sometimes we are so caught up in routine that the enormous inventory of things to be curious about fades completely into the background. Taking a few minutes to ignite a little ember of curiosity could do us good, but opening our minds to a practically endless list of researchable topics can leave us feeling overwhelmed. We're left wondering where we should start or how we would possibly organize a deeper dive into the plethora of possible material. It can seem daunting to know where to begin a curiosity trek, but the important thing to remember is that it doesn't necessarily matter where you look or what you learn; it's the process of sparking new parts of your brain that matters.

Research has shown that people with high levels of curiosity also have lower levels of stress and a greater contentment with life. Indulging our curiosity can help stave away various diseases that affect the memory, and it can also make us brilliant conversationalists. Taking a few moments a day to absorb new information can come in handy when there's a lull in a discussion. We all know someone who seems to be a fountain of knowledge, and that person probably seems that way thanks to a daily diet of random facts. Worried you won't remember them? You *will* remember things that are relevant to you, and something you learn on a curiosity hunt may even give you a brand new perspective on an old problem or an idea for a new business venture.

I used to do lectures for senior residences, and I was always looking for new topics. I found I was just as fascinated as they were. Captivating stories can be found in all kinds of subject matter. Some topics I covered were: US presidents, undersea life, the animal kingdom, various countries, movie stars, musicians, the stories behind particular songs, people who overcame poverty, how the states got their names, how different organs in the body function, inventions, and the origins of words. There wasn't one topic I researched that did not at some point elicit a big WOW!

We are so lucky to live in a time when this information is right at our fingertips, but searches don't always have to involve the internet. Those of a certain age will remember going to the library and checking out a pile of books in order to write a research paper. There's something that feels good about cracking open a book, an encyclopedia, or even just a newspaper and soaking up the information within. I have a 724-page book by Bernard Grun called *The Timetables of History*. It lists, in column form, what was going on in the world from 4500 B.C. to 1990. I can view, side by side, what was happening in any given year in the areas of politics, art, and society. Five minutes a day gives me a thoughtful perspective on my current world.

I once got curious about who had taught my college cello professor. I Googled it, and that led me through a chain of information about who taught the teacher before that and before that. At the end of it I had a string of teachers showing my cello roots all the way back to the 1700s. I was able to show my students where their musical knowledge originated in a sort of cello teacher "family tree." How often do we think about the evolution that various knowledge went through before reaching our own generation?

Curiosity also causes us to be more engaged with others, which leads to better relationships and enhanced performance at work, as well as improved academic achievement. When we show curiosity about the people we serve, we are better equipped to meet their needs. It can also help us avoid mistaken assumptions and inappropriate responses. If we know that someone has a sick child at home or is worried about an achy tooth, we might have more patience than we would otherwise.

Curiosity about people helps us expand our empathy for others. When we know someone on a more personal level, our prejudices tend to die away, and we treat each other differently. It may be initially awkward to ask questions of a person you don't know well, but it's amazing how often the conversation leads to something the two of you have in common or to some way you can both benefit from knowing each other. This is especially true with our older generations. We tend to see them as one uninteresting collective whose time has passed. This is tragic. The amount of rich experiences stored inside the brain of someone who's lived longer than half a century is astounding. One of my favorite things to do is to converse with an elderly person, whether I know that person or not. Retirement centers offer volunteer opportunities to chat with the residents. Nothing compares with hearing a first-hand account of being a stunt double for Shirley Temple, building the Reunion Tower in Dallas, getting smuggled past the Berlin Wall buried under coal in a delivery truck, or retrieving bodies from a battle zone.

Curiosity isn't restricted to the collection of knowledge. It's also rewarding to add to our warehouse of skills. I've often heard adults say, "I'm too old to learn to play the cello," or "It's too late for me to learn to paint." Some people limit themselves by type: "I'm not the athletic type." "I'm not the bookish type." The limits are in our own heads; we just haven't explored the possibilities. Allowing yourself even just ten minutes a day for curiosity will stretch you farther than you thought possible.

My son displaying curiosity at age two

☑ Try This

☐ Google a topic that has always piqued your interest.

☐ Look up the history of something in your town, such as a building, street name, or founding family.

☐ Take something apart and try to put it back together.

☐ Learn a new skill, even if you only take a couple of lessons. If you can't afford to hire a teacher, take advantage of the vast resources on the internet. Learn to dance, sing, play an instrument, do carpentry, fix a leaky faucet, speak a foreign language, make a bullet journal, or plant a garden. The possibilities are endless!

☐ Study up on a country that has always

intrigued you. What are its customs and cultures?

☐ Read the biography or autobiography of an inspiring person.

☐ Find out the backgrounds of your favorite songs.

☐ Pick a year and research things that happened during that year.

☐ Find archived newspapers or magazines online and read what happened on today's date in the past.

☐ Find out the history of different holidays or follow the National Days calendar. There's a different holiday for every day of the year.

☐ Pick an occupation and research its evolution. When did the first car insurance agent appear? Who was the first plumber?

☐ Ask for a behind-the-scenes tour at a theater, factory, or other institution.

☐ Explore other careers through a job shadow.

☐ Research a particular invention.

☐ In the interest of understanding others, learn more about a religion besides your own.

☐ Explore a museum you've never visited.

☐ Interview family members and find out more about them and the family history.

☐ Study alongside your children, grandchildren, nieces and/or nephews.

☐ Get to know your co-workers and clients. What things are important to them?

☐ Volunteer at a senior residence and converse with an elder. There are many books that serve as autobiography starters that can spark conversation. You may be helping someone fight loneliness.

Use Your Imagination

3

REMEMBER WHEN YOU could entertain yourself with just a box? It could become a pirate ship, a puppet theater, or a rocket to the moon. I remember making a refrigerator box into a gypsy fortune-telling booth that shot out little cards bearing answers to people's questions. I also spent a lot of time pretending to be Cinderella, particularly when my mother asked me to do chores.

Adults call this daydreaming, and it is typically frowned upon, but it's having a comeback in the form of vision boards and visualization meditation. Books such as *The Secret* and *Think Like a Millionaire* claim that truly feeling yourself in your desired situation is the key to attaining your heart's desires. Believing we have already received positive outcomes is the first step to getting them. We do that all the time as children.

I'll bet most of us at one point have fastened a towel around our neck and pretended to be a super hero. My brother and I took it a step farther and made a homemade zip line in the backyard. At some point it becomes uncool to pretend you're a superhero, but maybe it's not so crazy to try it as an adult. Some success coaches advise that in order to feel confident in intimidating situations such as giving a speech or asking for a raise, you should stand outside the room for a few moments and take the "Wonder Woman" stance: feet apart, head erect, and hands on hips. This, they assure, will give us an air of confidence. It's called "power posing," and studies have shown that it works. Researchers have found that holding such a pose for just five minutes can raise levels of testosterone and decrease stress hormones.

There are other benefits of pretending to be someone else for a while. Sometimes it's just nice to break your routine. Maybe that's why some people are so enamored with masquerade parties, Renaissance festivals, and Comic Cons.

The kids in my family frequently urge me to play along on some fantasy. As adults we tend to resist such antics, but kids seem to understand that it is natural and even healthy to let our brains transport us to another place.

As a teacher, I've noticed that the middle-school years are the age when the ability to imagine seems to fade. I've taken my son to Disney World at several stages in his life, and I remember a sad conversation we had when he was 13. He said, "Mom, I used to be able to pretend I was Peter Pan flying over London, and I can't do it anymore. Now I'm noticing the tracks above us, and I can see the cracks in the scenery." He wanted to get his imagination back, but he didn't know how.

When marveling at the architecture at Disney World or Universal Studios, my son often asked, "Why don't we build houses like this in real life? It would make life so much more fun!" I agreed that I didn't want the spell to be broken when we returned home, so I was always coming up with interesting ways to decorate his room. Once, I draped his ceiling in scallops of blue cellophane and hung plastic fish to create an undersea kingdom. Another time, I covered his ceiling in blue paint and glow-in-the-dark stars and dangled puffs of pillow stuffing for clouds, interspersed with hanging airplanes and birds. My most creative attempt was a Medieval room, with "stained-glass" windows, tapestries, and a revolving bookcase that opened to reveal a hidden chamber (the closet).

My son went on to design his own rooms (the jungle room was amazing), and now in his adulthood he is known for being able to transform even the tiniest space into a whimsical wonder of interior design. I wonder why as adults we tend to settle for the typical bland tans and browns in our interior and exterior home designs, seldom venturing into the extraordinary. Most of us are not very adventurous with our wardrobes, either. I've always admired the ladies of the Red Hat Society for trying to bring whimsy and color to their lives.

I know a woman who dresses up as a fairy godmother and visits children in the hospital. I can't help but think they heal a little faster after she has waved her magic wand over them. There is a hilarious magician named Lioz Shem Tov who performs "magic" using ordinary objects, pulling endless Kleenexes from a tissue box, making a wastebasket magically open with his foot, and making soap bubbles "disappear" in his hand. His act is a reminder that we can see magic in everything around us.

The movie *Life is Beautiful* is an excellent example of a parent using the power of imagination as he tries to shield his young son from the horrors of the Holocaust by turning it into an adventurous game. We shouldn't limit the benefits of imagination to children; sometimes adults need to be transported somewhere else too.

I never dreamed I would imagine myself as a character in my adulthood, but in 2012 it helped save me from despair. My brother was in a terrible accident that resulted in a traumatic brain injury. I was staying 24/7 in his hospital room for several weeks, and I was seeing some awful things. I could feel myself coming apart at the seams. One day I decided to imagine I was a robot monitoring my brother's room, and it actually helped me get myself under control. I repeated the technique each time I felt my nerves unravelling.

Sometimes using our imagination allows us to be more present or gives us a fresh perspective. When I am getting caught up in my problems, I stop what I'm doing and pretend to be an alien visiting Earth for the first time. Suddenly my problems seem foreign and even trivial compared to the scope of the Universe. Or if I'm being particularly harsh on myself with negative self-talk, I pause and pretend that instead of talking to myself, I am talking to a friend. This transforms my self-shaming into positive advice.

Imagination can improve relationships. If you can put yourself in other people's shoes and imagine what it's like to be them, you are more likely to empathize with them. You are more observant, more collaborative, and less combative. Imagination can help us solve problems by seeing things from a new perspective. Daydreaming about different outcomes helps us come up with solutions.

Do you ever get the feeling after you come out of a movie that you are in a movie yourself? For me it only lasts a few minutes, but as I'm throwing away my popcorn box or driving out of the parking lot, it kind of feels as if I'm still watching things through the camera's lens. When I go to the movies or read a novel, I often put myself in the place of the main character. Sometimes this feeling overlaps into my daily life, and instead of going through the day as Laurie Gabriel, I am Lara Croft conquering obstacles or Hermione Granger casting a spell.

Characters don't have to be fictional to inspire. Sometimes I draw from the talents of my friends. When I come across a problem, I think of my more resilient friends and ask myself what they would do. I often model myself after friends who are more organized, optimistic, outgoing, athletic, or compassionate than I.

Sometimes instead of imagining I am another person, I go through a day imagining that someone from my family is there with me, watching me. I'll pick someone—my mom, my son, or maybe my grandmother who's passed away—and imagine them at my side. Somehow it gives me a different perspective on my day. I might even behave better imagining they can see me. I forget I'm doing this as I get distracted with the details of the day, but I set the home screen on my phone with their picture, and it reminds me throughout the day.

Another person I bring with me for a day is myself from another age. I'll choose 15-year-old me, or college me, or maybe even 90-year-old me, and give them a tour of my life for a day. This is a real perspective changer. When your life is feeling really mundane, seeing it through the eyes of your younger self can give you a sense of gratitude and pride for how far you've come. Or if you're seeing yourself through the eyes of future you, you might think twice about eating that cupcake or using that credit card.

Have you ever imagined you're in a different place? Most of us have had some sort of beach or waterfall screen saver. I try taking that imagined destination a step further. When I go out for a walk or a drive, I try to convince my brain that I am in another place. Sometimes music helps the mood. I'll play international music while I'm driving somewhere and imagine I'm in the corresponding country. I seek out themed restaurants and other locales like Japanese gardens where I can pretend I'm not in the Dallas suburbs.

The imagined destination could also be a different place in time. I'll go to a museum that's set in an old house and imagine I live during the turn of the century, or I'll wander through a contemporary art museum and pretend I'm in some future realm. It sounds crazy, but it can be a wonderful escape from worry or routine.

The best part about imagination is that no one needs to know you are doing it except you. It's your own little secret.

My son in a "time-traveling tunnel"

☑ Try This

☐ Choose a favorite character from a movie or book and imagine you are that person for a day.

☐ Stare at a painting for five minutes and imagine you are inside the picture.

☐ Pretend you are an alien visiting from outer space. What is Earth like from that perspective?

☐ Pretend you are yourself from some past age visiting your own future (the present). What would amaze your past self about your life today? Try different past ages for different results.

☐ Hang out in a college library and imagine you are back in school. Remember the hope and optimism you felt at that time.

☐ Spend a day pretending you are in Hobbiton, Gotham City, Narnia, Neverland, or Wonderland; or pretend you are living in a different time period.

☐ Pretend you are a superhero with a secret power. Maybe that power could be something you're working on, like being outgoing, athletic, or courageous.

☐ Imagine that you have a fairy godmother or guardian angel watching over you all day. Maybe she'll make her presence known.

☐ Spend a day imagining that you are giving a tutorial on your life to someone. Imagine them learning from you as you go through your day.

☐ Make a list of ten friends whom you admire. Refer to the list when you want to imagine what they would do in some problematic situation you are experiencing.

☐ Imagine what you want your life to be like five or ten years from now and try to summon the feelings that go with that life.

☐ Spend a day pretending you are magic. Automatic doors open at your command. Your car is a flying contraption. Your coat is an invisibility cloak. Your pen is a magic wand. You can turn on the TV from across the room.

☐ Escape to a theme park and try to get caught up in childlike glee.

☐ Go to one of the new VR experiences where you can virtually walk through a different land.

☐ Go to an escape room and imagine you are really in the situation.

☐ Make a fairy garden (there are many supplies available in craft stores).

☐ Volunteer to read books to a kindergarten class and become the characters as you read.

☐ Join an improv troupe or take an acting class. Or buy plays and read them out loud using different voices for each character.

☐ Wear some type of clothing that you can imagine as a costume. It can be subtle—an ascot, a hat, or some sparkly shoes.

☐ Go to a Renaissance festival, Comic Con, or Cosplay convention. Dress up and play the part.

Be Creative

4

I OFTEN HEAR friends say they wish they could be creative. I truly believe all people are creative; they just may not have tapped into it yet. Some people don't begin to try because they feel their creation will be imperfect or inferior. You must banish all thoughts of trying to make something perfect. You don't even have to show it to anyone. The goal is to try.

At what moment do we decide we aren't able to create things simply because not everyone's skills are identical? Being creative is not just about painting pictures or writing music. Being creative means you are putting things together in a new way or manifesting something that wasn't there before. You are being creative when you use your keys to rip open a Frito bag, or when you use your briefcase to replace your forgotten umbrella. Many creative ideas have come about because people who lack the funds for certain things find ways to make cheaper alternatives for themselves.

Creativity also means solving problems by trying something no one else has tried. Many a new business has been born (or jetted to the top of its industry) by doing something the competitor hadn't thought of doing.

I love the Jennifer Lawrence movie *Joy*, in which the titular character starts out as a child making whimsical paper pop-ups and later in life ends up inventing a mop (as a solution to a problem) that changes the trajectory of her life. Equally compelling is the story of J.K. Rowling, who created the entire world of Harry Potter while trying to figure out how she was going to pay her bills.

So many of the things that exist on this planet are there because someone allowed his creative juice to flow. As a former teacher, I worry that schools do not dedicate enough time to letting students create things on their own rather than spend the bulk of their time memorizing things that other people have already figured out. We will need strong problem solvers for the future we have in store.

Embracing creativity can also make our lives more joyful (and a lot less boring). Many people complain about the mundane nature of their jobs. Loosening the reins to allow for more personal creativity from employees can boost productivity and morale. When our innate desire to create is squelched, our energy and motivation are diminished.

Creativity is a muscle that can be exercised and strengthened. It might not be easy to suddenly turn on creativity at a work meeting or social gathering, but if you start with little things, like setting aside ten minutes to doodle a picture or plunk out a melody on a piano, creativity will start to seep into other areas of your life.

I love the new popularity of **adult coloring books**. I was doing this before it was cool. As a teacher I used to keep a Barbie coloring book in my desk, and when I had a particularly rough class, I would pull out the crayons for five minutes and reset my emotions. You don't have to be an artist. Craft stores have projects and materials for every experience level. Pinterest is another great place to go for inspiration. It's amazing how many things you can create out of common household items. Take some ideas and put your own spin on them.

Creativity doesn't just apply to art projects. Walt Disney—the king of creativity—was continually asking, "How can we plus it?" He was always looking for ways to make his already impressive projects even more appealing or more enjoyable. You can look for ways to make things more interesting and visually appealing in your meals, home decor, wardrobe, or just about anything. It simply requires tapping into your old childhood brain.

When I traveled to Tokyo, I was impressed with how much care is given in Japan to visual appeal. It's in their architecture, their fashions, their Zen gardens, and their food presentation. It was like stepping into a wonderland. I particularly liked the little bento box meals, which were almost too pretty to eat.

Do you remember when you used to play with your food before you ate it? Did you form the peas into shapes or spell words with your alphabet soup noodles? I remember being told in my high-school home economics class that I should try to have at least three different colors on my plate, and I should arrange the food in an attractive design.

Yes, it does take a little bit of extra time to place your orange slices in a circle, but if you start thinking this way with the small things, it can spill into your work and your parenting as you look for little ways to make the day more delightful.

Creative writing is another outlet we tend to overlook. It can be hard to make time for this, but even five minutes of writing can be a big stress release. There are plenty of books and online resources that provide quick writing prompts; just choose one and write for five minutes. Though it does take longer, writing with a pen and paper is preferable to typing. You're more exposed to critical thinking when you write by hand than when you type. Handwriting gives you time to think more thoroughly about what you're writing. It encourages you to expand upon your thoughts and form connections between them.

Sometimes I write my worries on one side of a page, and on the other side I write from the viewpoint of an advisor solving my problems. Try to exercise your writing skills in both journaling and fiction. Pick a writing prompt from a book or online and write something that is true; then respond to the same prompt by writing something that is completely false. Doing this will exercise different areas of your brain and will boost your creativity in other areas.

Or you can create music, even if you're not a musician. Purchase an inexpensive plastic recorder, learn the basics on YouTube, and start tooting your own compositions. If you're really feeling ambitious, you can make a song out of your worries. I have a friend who does this with karaoke tracks. You can find instrumental blues backgrounds, or even just drum loops online, and sing your worries in the form of lyrics. It can be as goofy as you like. I wrote this about things that actually happened:

> I got coffee on my blouse (ba da da dum)
> No time to change (ba da da dum)
> All throughout the day today
> People will see the stain
> I got the blues—I got the blues real bad
> Somebody tell me—why I didn't wear plaid?

I sent out a text (ba da da dum)
To the wrong name (ba da da dum)
It was a poo emoji
Now I **look** insane
I got the blues—I got the blues real bad
I sent it to my boss when I thought it was my dad!

Even if you don't use a background track, singing your frustrations out loud can diminish them. If my boss does something to stress me out, I go into my car on my break and write an impromptu song about it. Sometimes if I have a student acting up, I completely throw him off by singing in my best opera voice: "What are you doing? Put that down!" Try this when you're having a fight with a family member. It will hopefully cut the tension! It's hard to sing and be angry at the same time, unless maybe you're singing heavy metal. Try that too!

My son about to get creative with some eggs

☑ Try This

☐ Make homemade greeting cards using paper collages, ink stamps, glitter glue, or feathers.

☐ Use online tutorials to learn how to paint with watercolors, oils, or acrylics, or buy a sketchbook that gives you starter instructions for drawing.

☐ Get some Play-Doh (or make your own), and make some sculptures.

☐ Cut things out from folded paper: snowflakes, hearts, or chains of people.

☐ Learn to fold origami shapes.

☐ Make an artistic scrapbook of clippings, photos, and other mementos.

☐ Scour Pinterest for homemade craft ideas.

☐ Subscribe to magazines about decorating, gardening, crafting, cooking, or art.

☐ Make designs with your food. It can be something as simple as arranging your pretzel sticks into a star shape. If you want to get ambitious, Google bento boxes and go for it!

☐ Put together an outfit using clothing items you wouldn't normally combine.

☐ Rearrange your furniture or decorate a room in a whimsical way.

☐ Play charades, Pictionary, Cranium, or other games that stimulate creativity.

☐ Read the book *How To Think Like Leonardo da Vinci* or look up biographies of other inventors.

☐ Come up with an invention and consider getting it patented.

☐ Think of a problem in your workplace, city, or world, and brainstorm solutions. Write down as many as you can think of in ten minutes. Pick a couple to try.

BE CREATIVE

☐ Look up one of the many resources for making an inspiring bullet journal.

☐ Throughout the day, notice things that are amusing and write them down so you can turn them into jokes.

☐ Find resources for writing prompts and write fictional or true answers, or keep a daily journal and try writing it from various points of view: humorous, third-person narrative, soap-opera style, etc.

☐ Write your day out as a script with different characters. You can try this for the day you just had or for the day you want to have tomorrow.

☐ Write a melody with lyrics or come up with a rap. Perform it for your pets.

☐ Try your hand at haiku, limericks, or other forms of poetry.

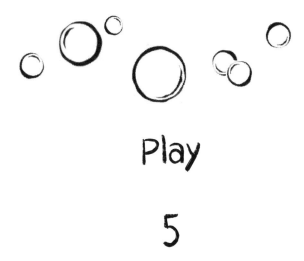

Play

5

I ONCE HAD the opportunity to interview Nancy Carlsson-Page, an expert in play (yes, there is such a thing). She expressed concern over the trend in public schools to reduce recess time in favor of more academics. Ms. Carlsson-Page, author of *Taking Back Childhood,* has spent years studying play and its importance to learning.

Play is the most crucial vehicle children have for building ideas, growing socially, and working out emotional needs. Children should not be spending the majority of their free time in front of screens. This practice results in children simply imitating what they are seeing on the screen, to the detriment of inventive play in which children write their own scripts.

Similarly, when schools emphasize teacher-led learning rather than a corroborative process as is seen in play, children do not have the opportunity to nurture the skills that organically arise during play. In this era of focus on testing and standards, play is being eliminated. This is a sad trend.

When my mother was a special-education teacher, she was admonished for allowing a twelve-year-old boy to swing on a swing set, which was the only thing that made him laugh. She was told it was not age-appropriate and was warned that it should not happen again.

Play is not just for children. For both kids and adults, play should be a time of guilt-free stress release, a chance for community without expectations, and a reminder of what's really important. What good are the fruits of your labor if you're not going to enjoy them?

Countries such as Austria and Australia have figured out that allowing their workers paid vacation time helps prevent burnout. Austria has a legal minimum of twenty-two paid vacation days each year, plus thirteen paid holidays. Australia is close behind with twenty required paid vacation days and ten paid holidays. By law, every country in the European Union has at least four weeks of paid vacation time. Happy citizens make for happy businesses, happy communities, and happy countries.

In contrast, the United States is the only developed country in the world without a single legally required paid vacation day or holiday. According to the Bureau of Labor Statistics, the average American worker has to be employed for one year before receiving paid time off, after which the average is ten days of vacation. The average US employee also clocks twenty percent more hours per worker than those in Europe. Is it any wonder so many Americans report feeling exhausted?

Even when Americans are given vacation days, an estimated 52 percent of workers do not use them, because they are afraid of falling behind in their work. According to Project: Time Off in a 2019 report, more than 700 million vacation days go unused each year in the United States, representing 66.4 million dollars in lost benefits.

What those who forfeit their vacations may not understand is that true productivity isn't measured in hours. In fact, fewer hours may even be good for productivity. According to a 2017 study in *Fortune* magazine, employees who forfeited vacation time were less likely to have been promoted within the last year or to have received a raise or bonus in the last three years.

Innovation expert Mitch Ditkoff has interviewed 10,000 people over the last 30 years about where they get their best ideas, and less than two percent of them said it happened at work. Cases in point: Howard Schultz, creator of Starbucks, and Lin Manuel Miranda, writer of the musical *Hamilton*, both say they got their best ideas while on vacation.

Companies like Google, Pandora and Yeti have figured out that allowing their employees time for play not only increases creativity and productivity, it attracts more desirable applicants.

Some of the perks of working for Google include Lego play areas, scavenger hunts, massages, yoga, art easels, board games, comfy reading areas, whimsical cafes, and even allowances for pets to come to work.

Google's engineering director, Craig Neville-Manning, explains that this philosophy makes people want to come to work and collaborate, rather than dreading every Monday. I don't think anyone can question the success of Google, and if you're doubting Nancy Carlsson Page's philosophy of play over testing, take note that her son turned out pretty well. He's Matt Damon.

How often do you put off having fun? Yes, we all need to work hard, but balance is important. By balance I don't necessarily mean equal amounts of work and play; that would be difficult to pull off. However, some of us struggle to allow even five minutes a day to do something silly and spontaneous. Start with five minutes a day and see where it takes you.

My son on his favorite piece of playground equipment

☑ Try This

☐ Revisit some of your favorite outdoor childhood activities, like jump-roping, hopscotch, Frisbee, kick the can, jacks, or marbles.

☐ Find a playground and use the equipment. Swing on the swings, slide down the slide, and hang from the monkey bars.

☐ Ride a bicycle, scooter, or hoverboard.

☐ Skip down the sidewalk or roll down a hill. Run through a sprinkler.

☐ Sled in the snow, ice skate, build a snow fort, or have a snowball fight.

☐ Find a sandbox and put your feet in it or build a sandcastle.

☐ Master the yo-yo.

PLAY

☐ Learn some simple magic tricks.

☐ Learn a silly dance online.

☐ Play a board game or do a jigsaw puzzle.

☐ Make a paper airplane and see how far it will fly, or find a place to skip stones on the water.

☐ Go to an amusement park or find a miniature golf course.

☐ Color in a coloring book or do some finger-painting.

☐ Do sudoku or word puzzles.

☐ Play tennis, handball, racquetball or pickleball, or simply bounce a ball against a wall.

☐ Go bowling or swimming.

☐ Watch cartoons instead of the news.

☐ Put together a model airplane.

☐ Make jewelry out of beads.

☐ Build a blanket fort or pitch a tent in your backyard.

☐ Visit a museum, zoo, or aquarium.

☐ Play with a dog, cat, or other animal.

Appreciate Nature

6

HOW LONG CAN a kid entertain himself sitting by a stream or playing in a pile of leaves? Hours! Do you remember getting completely caught up in nature when you were a child? What sorts of activities made you lose all sense of time?

I used to love cracking rocks open or watching ants carrying stuff. Sometimes we forget we have access to this 24/7 for free! Think you're too busy? Five minutes is all you need for a reset. Go outside when you need a release and find some piece of nature in which to immerse yourself. It could be a leaf, a bug, or clouds; just stare intently for five minutes, and you'll be amazed at how quickly your stress vanishes. If you can't get outside, keep a piece of nature indoors. When you need a break, pull out your shell, pinecone, or stone and simply look at it, wondering how it came to be. Or keep a vase of fresh flowers at your desk and count the petals when you're getting stressed.

We need to be reminded often how mind-boggling nature is. It makes us care more about it. When I was little, I was horrified when I saw trash on the ground. I had to pick it up immediately and put it in the right place. I don't know exactly when it happened, but I reached a point where I just didn't notice the litter anymore. But when I'm thinking like my childhood self, I bring a grabby stick and a bag when I go on walks. On one short stroll through my neighborhood, I gathered enough garbage to fill a kitchen-sized trash bag.

We seem to care a lot more about the environment when we are little. There is a popular YouTube video showing a little boy in his car seat who is beside himself with grief over how adults are treating the environment. Through his sobs, he vows to protect the rainforest when he grows up. What if we all felt so passionately about our home?

APPRECIATE NATURE

When I was a kid, I went around the neighborhood with a clipboard gathering signatures to save the whales. I desperately needed to make other people care about the whales. You may have had a similar campaign. But as we get older, a lot of us give up. We feel as if no one else is doing anything to save the planet, so what's the use? We don't think our singular efforts are going to make a difference. But kids see things the opposite way; if *they* care about something, surely they can get someone else to care about it too. Greta Thunberg cared about it so much she sailed all the way from Sweden to the United States to make her voice heard at the UN Climate Action Summit. It would be a shame to leave environmental concerns to younger people. We ought to be right in there with them.

I don't know why our advocacy for the planet tends to fade as we get older, but I suspect it is just a gradual numbing of our sensitivity to the awesomeness of nature's wonders. A friend of mine used to walk to work daily in Brooklyn. One day she mentioned her route to a co-worker. "Oh, that street has the most beautiful blossoming trees at this time of year," said the co-worker. My friend realized she'd walked on that street for five spring seasons and never really stopped to look at those trees. On her way home that day, she couldn't believe the beauty she had overlooked. She started leaving for work ten minutes earlier each day so she could walk slowly and take in the scenery.

Perhaps if it were mandatory to spend time in nature every day, our concern for it would stay at the forefront of our thoughts. Maybe if we were required to view information about our struggling planet (or listen to what children have to say about it), we would be more inclined to take action.

If we are in the presence of a suffering animal, it is difficult to turn our backs to it. A BBC film crew that was making a documentary about penguins broke its "do not interfere" rule when they saw some baby penguins trapped in a ravine. Unable to watch the animals suffer, the crew jumped into action and built a ramp to help the penguins get free.

How many times a day do we think about the animals that are going extinct on our planet? More than 99 percent of the five billion species that ever lived on Earth are estimated to have died out. Habitat degradation caused by agriculture, urban sprawl, logging, mining, and pollution is the main cause of species extinction. Biologist E. O. Wilson estimated in 2002 that if current rates of human destruction of the biosphere continue, half of all plant and animal species on Earth will be extinct in 100 years.

Intervention can help. Giant pandas were downgraded from "endangered" to "vulnerable" after massive breeding efforts resulted in a turnaround. We just have to decide it is important.

Plant life needs our help as well. Every minute, trees covering the space of 20 football fields are cut down. Half the world's tropical forests have already been cleared. It is estimated that within 100 years there will be no rainforests left. Loss of forests contributes significantly to greenhouse gas emissions, resulting in climate change and extreme temperature swings.

One solution is to reduce the demand for paper. We in the USA are in a strong position to make a difference. Though we comprise only five percent of the world's population, we consume more than thirty percent of the world's paper supply. On average, a person in the United States uses more than 700 pounds of paper every year. Much of our paper waste is caused by junk mail and wasteful packaging.

We humans make up just .01 percent of all living things, yet we control in large part whether or not *all* the other species will survive. If we could see our world through the eyes of the children who will inherit it, perhaps we could increase our level of care for what is happening to our beautiful home.

Trash collected on a
short neighborhood walk

☑ Try This

☐ Spend five minutes staring at a flower or a leaf. Marvel at its intricacies.

☐ Watch a bug crossing the sidewalk or a bird soaring through the air. Meditate on the fact that you both share the planet equally.

☐ Bring a small piece of nature to your desk each week or carry one around in your pocket. Pick it up and look at it when you need a breather.

☐ Walk barefoot in some grass.

☐ Sit next to a waterfall or other body of water.

☐ Park a few blocks from work and walk the rest of the way. Change where you park each day. Notice nature as you walk.

APPRECIATE NATURE

☐ Eat lunch under a tree.

☐ Find a hiking trail. Get maps for your area online or at the Visitors' Bureau.

☐ Each time you go for a walk, carry a bag and a grabber tool and pick up trash. Consider adopting a neighborhood.

☐ Watch documentaries about ecology.

☐ Plant a garden or tree.

☐ Carpool, ride your bike, use public transportation, or consider a hybrid or electric vehicle.

☐ Write to your political representatives concerning environmental mistreatment.

☐ Support state and national parks by visiting them and paying the entry fee.

☐ Recycle.

☐ Use refillable water bottles and reusable shopping bags.

☐ Make an effort to reduce junk mail by asking to be taken off of catalog lists.

☐ Choose products that require less packaging.

☐ "Adopt" an animal at a nature preserve and pay for its yearly care, or contribute to a conservation effort.

☐ Adopt a pet from a shelter.

See Everyone as a Friend

7

HAVE YOU EVER had some little kid just come up to you and start telling you a story as if you were lifelong friends? What is it about a child's mind that removes all inhibitions about talking to other people? True, they are sometimes shy and hide behind a parent's leg, but it often doesn't take much for them to break down walls and befriend anyone who will have them.

I once saw two kids in an airport coming toward each other from different directions. They both looked as though they had learned to walk the previous week. As they got closer to each other, without making a sound, they dropped their tiny rolly bags, hugged it out, then gathered their little suitcases and continued on their separate ways. They seemed thrilled at the idea of encountering a fellow toddler and had no problem expressing it.

My mom says when I was little I used to go around the grocery store calling every man I encountered "Daddy." I don't imagine that would go over well if I did it today, but I do often wish I could tap into that extroverted version of myself and just regard everyone as a friend.

Wouldn't it be great if we all saw ourselves simply as members of the same species, tackling our collective problems and fears and trying to survive another day on this spinning ball of clay? After all, it's pretty amazing that in this gigantic universe, we have all landed together on this little speck of a planet for reasons unknown.

A funny thing happens when you travel. It suddenly becomes fascinating when you stumble across a traveler from the city where you live. "YOU'RE FROM DENVER??? I'M FROM DENVER!!!" When we're in Denver, we couldn't care less if we meet another person from Denver, but if we meet in New Zealand, suddenly we feel a bond. I wonder if we'll ever find ourselves traveling through space and get all excited when we meet someone from Earth.

We also don't seem to have a problem finding kinship with our fellow sports fans. All you have to do is wear the right jersey in the right place, and you're immediately in a "club." Unfortunately, many of our bonds don't go much deeper than a superficial commonality, because some of us would rather eat our shoes than carry a conversation deeper than sports or the weather. We are reluctant to delve into things that really matter. We don't want to be that person who starts a conversation on an elevator. We don't want to talk to a neighbor. What if the conversation drags on and on, or we're asked inside? What if the person asks us for help with something? We don't have time!

True, there aren't enough hours in the day to hear all the stories of all the people we encounter, but what if making a slight shift in that direction could be a game changer in our world climate?

I teach private cello lessons. My job is to

show my students how to master an instrument. But sometimes those kids just want to tell me something. One of my students showed up for his lesson without his glasses. I asked him, "Where are your glasses?" He said someone had taken his glasses from his locker during gym and had etched the words YOU SUCK on the lenses. He knew who it was because the kid who did it had bragged about it. My student was frustrated because the adults he'd approached had not offered any help, merely telling him there was no proof of who did it and he should just drop it. I listened intently to him for the first ten minutes of his lesson and told him I shared his sadness and frustration. He thanked me for being the only person who seemed to care. Then we played the cello together. I don't know if that stopped him from some future act of frustrated rage, but I do wonder if there were moments in the lives of other students who did go down a path of revenge that could have been a turning point. Was some opportunity missed that would have sent them on a different trajectory?

When we hear the quotes from school shooters, many of them final words, there seems to be a theme. The kids who commit these tragic acts often say they felt that no one listened to them. No one came to their defense when they needed help. They were lonely. This does not excuse their behavior, but what if someone had taken the time to get to know them? Would it have saved lives? Wouldn't that be worth trying?

As a teacher, I used to tell myself I didn't have time to get to know my students. Truthfully, I was completely swamped with paperwork and data entry, but I had a few experiences that made me change my priorities. For instance, I discovered that a student who'd been in trouble for not turning in signed practice sheets could not get his sheets signed because one parent was in jail and the other was in the hospital. I found out that one student, whom I had admonished for missing a concert, had actually been busy winning a gold medal for skiing at the Junior Olympics in Switzerland. Who knows what hidden talents and histories are all around you, packed inside the people you have been working alongside for years, maybe even decades?

When we are familiar with people, we treat them differently. On my way to work one day, I got cut off by some rude guy in one of those expensive sports cars with dark tinted windows. I decided to speed ahead

and cut *him* off so he could see how it is.
I also honked at him, yelled some things out the window, and made a couple of bad gestures. Then the guy started following me. He was making every turn I made, right into the school parking lot. I was thinking, "Is this guy going to get out of the car and punch me?" Then I realized it was my principal pulling in to work. Because I knew him I was terribly embarrassed, but for some reason my behavior wasn't embarrassing when I thought he was a stranger.

Sometimes when a student is acting up, I take a moment and imagine that he or she is my own child, and I immediately feel a sense of compassion. What if we did this in all interactions? What if we held our fellow humans in the same regard that we hold our own family? We charge through life worrying about our own interests, as if the suffering of others has nothing to do with us; but the suffering of other humans affects us all, whether we are aware of it or not.

We tend to reserve our deepest care and concern for those in our close inner circles, but children cast the net much wider, even caring for inanimate objects. I love the YouTube video of the little boy who is getting ready to hit a Spiderman piñata with a bat. He wrestles with the idea until he drops the bat and runs over to give the piñata a big hug. Kids have to be taught to harm others or see them as inferior.

In certain cultures, such as India, Turkey and Russia, there are traditions in which people call each other the equivalent of brother or sister (or aunt or uncle if the person is older), even if the other person is a stranger. I like this acknowledgement that we are all members of the same human family.

Seeing others as friends can ease our fear of people we might ordinarily see as adversaries. Are you nervous about making sales calls, going for a job interview, or asking for a raise? Try imagining you're a child and the other person is just another kid with whom you'd like to toss a Frisbee. You're likely to be more relaxed. Do you start to feel uncomfortable when talking with someone from a different political party, religion, or culture? Try tapping into the childhood self who didn't let those things get in the way of friendship.

In these times of social media, it's tempting to "unfriend" people who post comments that reveal a different opinion from our own. I've had my finger hovering over the unfriend button a few times myself, but then I think about all the lost opportunities to discuss and resolve our issues rather than walk away. Fleeing the friendship simply lets the divisions widen.

It's also common for those in leadership roles to ignore the ideas and opinions of their subordinates, but doing so results in employees quitting or giving less than their best. Listening to employees gives them a sense of partnership, and this increases their loyalty and performance. This is something we innately know but seldom practice.

One of the big topics of the twenty-first century is the addition of SEL—social emotional learning—to public-school curriculum. The most important skill acquired in SEL is "theory of mind," or understanding the perspective of other people. We can't really do that if we are not engaging with each other.

The book *Habit*, by Charles Duhigg, details experiments showing that people are much more likely to help people they know than people they haven't met. They are also more likely to send funds to aid people in their own city than to send donations to a country on the other side of the planet. But if we each had a sense of connection to *all* humans and acknowledged that "neighbor" is a relative term, we might see progress toward a better world.

New-found airport buddies

☑ Try This

☐ Start a conversation with a complete stranger.

☐ Tell a joke on a crowded elevator.

☐ Spend a whole day finding out the names of the people you encounter, such as your mailman, your receptionist, or your grocery clerk. Call them by their names.

☐ Spend a day being certain to make eye contact with everyone with whom you have a conversation, however brief.

☐ Make it a monthly goal to find out something new about the people you see regularly. Do they have any hobbies? What jobs did they do before this one? What are their children like? Where have they traveled? What's going well for them? What are their struggles?

- [ ] Come up with more personal alternatives to "How are you?" Examples: "How's your daughter?" "How did that project end up?" "Did you golf again this weekend?"

- [ ] Invite someone for a tennis game, round of bowling, or board game night.

- [ ] Occasionally substitute a phone call for a text message or email.

- [ ] Have a get-together with one of your neighbors. Agree on a time limit if you are concerned about it taking up too much of your time.

- [ ] See how many people you can get to smile at you in one day.

- [ ] See how many people you can get to wave at you in one day.

- [ ] Let people into your traffic lane if they are signaling to do so.

- [ ] Let someone cut in front of you in line at the grocery store.

- [ ] Spend a day imagining that everyone you encounter is a family member or

SEE EVERYONE AS A FRIEND

friend. Superimpose the face of your mother onto a homeless person, or the face of your best friend onto a grouchy co-worker.

☐ Visit a church you don't normally attend and try to see the congregants simply as fellow humans rather than viewing them as people you wish shared your ideology.

☐ Attend a political gathering of a party that opposes your own and try to listen to their individual stories. Seek to understand.

☐ Engage in a conversation with a homeless person on the street. Let them know you see them.

☐ Read up on subjects about which you may have a closed mind. Look up stories of individual immigrants, women who had to end a pregnancy, people who have a different gender identity, or people who are addicted to drugs. Instead of passing judgment, try to understand their perspectives. Imagine them as your friends or family members and try to elicit genuine compassion for them.

☐ Engage in civil conversations with people on social media who don't share your agenda. Try to listen to them calmly and understand that their paths and experiences are not the same as yours. If you seek to persuade someone on an issue, try to do so without becoming angry or threatening to end the relationship.

☐ Don't forget about friends you haven't talked to for a while. Choose one per week or one per month and check in.

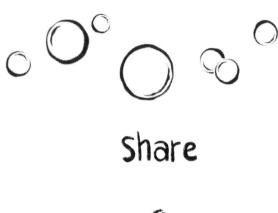

Share

8

THERE'S A STORY about a village in Africa where an anthropologist did an experiment with a culture he had been studying. He put together a basket of treats and set it under a tree. Then he gathered up the children in the village and drew a line in front of them in the dirt, telling them they were going to race for the basket. Whoever reached it first would receive all the treats. When he gave the signal for them to run, they took each other's hands and ran together to the tree. Then they sat around the basket and enjoyed their treat as a group. The anthropologist was shocked. He asked why they would all go together when one of them could have won all the treats for himself. A young girl looked up at him and said, "How can one of us be happy if all the other ones are sad?"

There are some who say that story is just a legend, but whether or not it is, I have seen this behavior firsthand from toddlers. Yes, we have all likely seen selfish toddlers clutching a toy crying, "MINE," but much more often we see toddlers walking up to people—sometimes complete strangers—and handing them things they want to share. Toddlers don't like to see their fellow humans upset.

I was once complaining in front of my five-year-old son about not having enough money. This prompted him to go to his room and return with his piggy bank, tenderly asking, "Will this help?" Toddlers don't have the mentality that helping someone else will take away from what they have.

We see many adults clamoring to have "the most" and "the best" at the expense of others. The goal seems to be to have the highest benefits for those at the top, even if the workers helping generate those profits can barely live on what they are paid. Thankfully, some companies are taking the initiative to reduce the gap in pay between CEOs and rank-and-file workers. They are realizing that when they invest in their people, their employees become more dedicated, and this benefits everyone.

As we seemed to understand when we were children, it's common sense that when each of us is happy, all of us are happy. There's got to be some kind of achievable balance where there is not so much disparity between those who have and those who do not have. What if we changed the mentality of aspiring to have more than everybody else? Would there be more satisfaction and less anxiety? Would we have to worry less about theft and crimes of desperation?

The predominant voices seem to say we must think only of ourselves and resist helping others. That will keep us on top. But will it? Imagine this kind of attitude in the school cafeteria. A kid barrels through the line wearing a shirt that says "Me First." He pushes other people out of the way and grabs all the food he can carry, eats just a little bit of it and throws the rest away. If someone falls down, he steps over them yelling, "Me first!" Do you think other people are going to look up to this person? Do you think people will jump in to assist him if he ever needs help?

If access to the Earth's resources were evenly distributed, all people in the world could live at a decent standard. Instead, we have some countries eating huge amounts and throwing away heaps of food while others go without. There are currently 87 countries that cannot produce the food they need, nor do they have the money to import it. Average Americans spend only 10 percent of their money on food and still buy so much they throw away 15 percent of it. Meanwhile in Africa, 3/4 of the population spend more than half their income on food and are still undernourished.

The same goes for other resources. Even though the US makes up only 4 percent of the world's population, we consume 25 percent of the world's energy, often wastefully. According to the United States Geological Survey, US citizens use 80–100 gallons of water per day, compared to countries such as Sengal, where the average water use is 7 gallons per day. Only 48 percent of Africans have access to safe water at all. Perhaps if we conserved more and used the resulting savings to help those in need, we could achieve more balance.

It's tempting to celebrate our prosperity by consuming just because we can. It can also be scary to share if we already feel a sense of scarcity. But it is important to see things from a realistic perspective. Wealth is relative. There is almost always someone who is in greater need than oneself. I have seen people with practically nothing who still find a way to share with someone else who is suffering, even if what they're offering (a hug, a kind word, or a shared space under a blanket) costs nothing.

We spend a lot of time comparing ourselves to everyone who makes more money than we do, and advertisements perpetuate the belief that we are constantly lacking. Most of us could probably examine our situation and find many things that fall into the "more than we really need" category. I admit that my attic is stocked with things that have spent the last ten years in a box instead of being used by someone who needs them. Many of those things are baby clothes and household goods that were donated to me when I needed assistance. It's time to pay them forward.

Sharing doesn't only apply to money and goods. Time can also be shared. In our overburdened lives, sharing time can seem tough, if not impossible. But when we consider the ripple effect that sharing our time can have on improving our societal climate, we become aware that the rewards far outweigh the cost. Sharing time with people in need can diminish problems like substance abuse or suicide. Modeling a desire to share time with a lonely elderly person might ensure that future generations will do the same for us. Most importantly, once we allow ourselves the experience, we realize that sharing just feels good.

My son sharing a favorite toy with his uncle

Try This

☐ Go through your closet, pick out items you rarely wear, and donate them.

☐ Sift through your garage and attic for unused items that might be someone else's treasure.

☐ Don't put usable items in the trash. Call a local charity to come pick them up.

☐ When grocery shopping, buy an extra canned item or two for the local food bank, or share excess food or flowers from your garden. When you bake cookies, put some aside as a surprise for someone else.

☐ Share time serving food at a local shelter.

☐ Help set up a Little Free Library or Little Free Food Pantry in your community.

☐ Join the Freecycle Network, which gives people access to each other's unwanted items.

☐ If you are an artist or musician, share your craft with someone who normally can't access it.

☐ Share a smile with everyone you meet today, or pass along your favorite joke.

☐ Share your expertise on a certain subject via YouTube, or share a recipe.

☐ Share time with an elderly person in an assisted-living facility. There are agencies that coordinate this.

☐ Share time reading to at-risk children. Ask your local school district or library how to set it up.

☐ Share time helping a disadvantaged young person through a mentoring program like the Boys and Girls Club of America.

☐ Share time raking leaves, shoveling snow, or putting up holiday lights for a neighbor.

☐ Figure out ways to ride-share.

☐ Donate to a worthy cause. Even $5 helps.

Don't Judge by Appearance

9

ISN'T IT INTERESTING that one of the things that occupies a major amount of our time and money is what to do with the strands of dead follicles that flow from our scalps? Hairstyles are the source of all kinds of angst from just about every generation, and they are also the source of over three billion dollars a year for the hair industry. We've got hair gels, pomades, mousses, sprays, shampoos, conditioners, hair dyes, growth enhancers, curl diminishers, curl enhancers, leave-in treatments, curling irons, flattening irons, hot rollers, blow dryers, barbers, hair stylists, hair removers, and hair transplant experts. All of this stems from our fear that our hair will not be approved by the general public. The fact that trends change frequently does not make matters easier. This has been going on since Ancient Egyptian times and beyond.

There are two lucky populations that escape this scrutiny: babies and people in their nineties. I like to think of it in terms of a line graph:

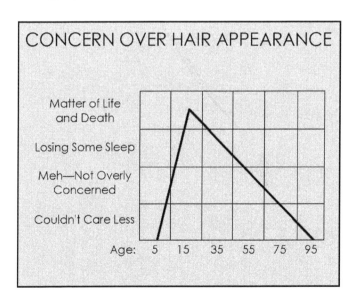

We don't typically see toddlers assessing one another's hairstyles or onesie labels. This is because they are not interested in each other's appearance. They just care about whether someone is nice or not nice. Just think how much time, grief, and money we could save if we were not so obsessed with judgments based on hairstyle, clothing, and possessions.

When does this tendency to rate our fellow humans by appearance start? Studies show that kids with older siblings learn to do this much earlier than their only-child peers, but we don't need older siblings to show us the ropes. We also learn it from our parents, from society, and from television shows like *America's Next Top Model*, where people are gradually eliminated until only the "best" human remains.

How many of us have stayed home from school, work, or a party just because we couldn't get our appearance to match up to a predetermined standard? How many of us have been late getting somewhere because we had to manage a cowlick or change our outfit?

It can be exhausting to be judged by so many different factors, but it can also be draining to be the judge. It doesn't feel very good to criticize the appearance of others, despite our efforts to convince ourselves otherwise. Something about it just feels wrong.

Judging by outward appearance isn't limited to hairstyle and fashion. Too many of us also judge others by their skin color, body size, or gender. This is no trivial matter. Throughout history, this has resulted in the murders, suicides and marginalization of millions of humans who were innocently trying to go about their days.

Unfortunately, we allow ourselves to be convinced by others that people who look a certain way are "nerds," or "lazy," or "ugly," or "terrorists," or "anti-social." Those toddlers who are organically accepting of others regardless of appearance have to be taught that people who don't look the "right" way should not be befriended. Sadly, this is being taught earlier and earlier, sometimes resulting in suicides at increasingly young ages. We seldom stop to consider what effect our words have on other people. Are judgmental words worth destroying a life?

Even when we call someone handsome, pretty, or stylish, we are reinforcing the idea that we place value on people's physical characteristics. Each time we hear a compliment about our body, face, hair, or clothes, it reinforces in our minds that we must strive to stand out in those areas. We could even start to think that our non-physical characteristics don't deserve as much attention as our physical ones. A well-meaning compliment about someone's looks could be seen as a dismissal of more substantive traits.

What if we focused on praising women's ideas, creativity, or contributions instead of their hair, makeup, clothing, face shapes, or body types? What if we celebrated men's honesty, kindness, and accomplishments instead of their full heads of hair, square jaws, or chiseled pecs?

Why do we place so much importance on physical standards and fashion trends? Do we really want every human being to look and dress alike? Of course not! Even so, we want to feel as though we are somehow "in" while others are, in contrast, "out." We want others to know that we know what's in fashion. Ironically, the reason we "know" what's in fashion is that we listen closely to what *others* tell us is *supposed* to be in fashion. The ability to keep up with where your hem should fall and how wide your pant leg should be somehow earns you a badge of honor in society. Knowing exactly the day of the year when it becomes permissible to wear white shoes makes a person superior to those who don't know. This would sound ridiculous to a toddler until someone else told him otherwise. What if we could return to our original state of not categorizing people by their appearance?

If there is one trait from childhood that we should cling to with everything we've got, it's the ability to move through life not caring about other people's outward appearance (or other superficial elements) and really focus on what's inside.

Perhaps a sense of community is the key. It tends to be the larger cities and schools where appearance seems most important. This is likely because compacted populations naturally feel a greater sense of competition. The smaller a community is, the less likely its members are to be swept away by each new trend. When we know other people on a deep friendship level, we understand how they arrived at who they are, and we care about them for their inner beauty, not for how they look. Striving to understand and accept all of our fellow humans rather than forming snap judgments could be our biggest hope for world peace.

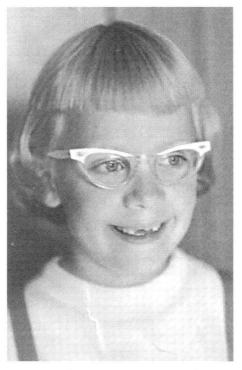

The author at the age when she first realized
appearance was going to be important

☑ Try This

☐ Keep a notebook with you and mark down the number of times you judge another person's appearance, whether it's silently or out loud. See if you can reduce the number each day until it's zero.

☐ Force yourself to go out of your house without makeup or in a mismatched outfit. Ponder how liberating it would be to not care about appearance.

☐ Step in if you hear someone criticizing another person's appearance. Say something like, "Well, I like her because she has great ideas and is super friendly."

☐ Get to know someone who looks different from you. If you can't do it in person, read a book or article about another culture, country, religion, or income class. Seek to understand all kinds of people from the inside out.

☐ When you find yourself about to judge another person's appearance, quickly switch to a predetermined behavior that disrupts that process. This gets easier with practice. Some of the predetermined behaviors could be:

- Picturing that person as one of your family members
- Saying a quick silent prayer
- Holding your breath and counting to five
- Tapping your foot ten times
- Reciting a short poem or song in your head
- Asking the person a friendly question

☐ Use the THINK model before you say anything: Is it True? Helpful? Inspiring? Necessary? Kind? If the answer is no, consider not saying it.

☐ Try listing positive attributes about people you know (or about celebrities) without including any physical traits.

☐ The next time you are going to praise someone's physical appearance, consider praising a non-physical attribute instead.

☐ The next time you are about to judge someone's appearance, ask yourself why it is important for you to do so.

☐ Take notice of ads that try to convince you to change your appearance or use images that equate their products with being attractive. Sometimes just being aware of how easily media manipulates us can put a stop to it.

☐ Make a list of stereotypes you or people you know typically hold about people who look a certain way. Begin to challenge those stereotypes.

☐ Search the internet for stories about people who have struggled with other people's comments about their weight, style choices, hair, or skin. Let yourself absorb what effect unkind words have had on their lives.

Show Your Feelings

10

I WAS ONCE in a restaurant with my Uncle Steff when a small child suddenly dropped to the floor and started having a loud temper tantrum because he didn't want to eat his spaghetti. Ever the comedian, my uncle dryly queried, "What if we all did that?" This conjured up a hilarious picture in my mind of all the adults in the restaurant spinning on the floor screaming because they didn't like their dinners.

By the time we reach age seven or so, the urge to fully and honestly express our feelings is socially conditioned out of us. There are reasons for this. It might be hard to be productive in a society where we all started crying every time we didn't want to do something. But is it possible we've gone too far in the other direction, holding our true feelings in until they explode in a shower of carnage? Suppression of our feelings can lead to burnout, substance abuse and other types of self-harm.

There are many books and workshops on the subject of learning how to say no. Perhaps a better phrase would be "*relearning* how to say no," as we had no problem doing that until people started telling us that saying no was unacceptable. These same people would confuse us by saying no to us until we stopped saying no.

It's important to speak up about what we want. One of the top causes of anxiety and depression in adults is that they feel they are "living someone else's life." They set aside their dreams in order to follow someone else's prescribed plans for their life. While the advice of those "someone elses" is well-meaning, it leaves a residual feeling inside the recipient that a dream was sacrificed, and that sentiment is bound to resurface one day.

Many a successful entrepreneur has lectured about how she "went with her gut," "took a leap of faith," or "followed her heart." Some may see this as irresponsible and flighty, and sometimes those leaps can end in a fall, but taking that leap is an important part of a life well lived. Interviews with people in their eighties and nineties usually contain advice about not worrying so much and just doing what you love.

Baby Boomers seem to be the generation for whom the "head first, heart second" rule applies. They see Globals and Millennials crafting lives that are easier than their own and mistakenly call them "lazy." Is following your bliss and making your life as stress-free as possible truly irresponsible? As long as we are not trampling on others on our way to our goals nor neglecting our families, I think it's best we go ahead and do those things we really want to do without guilt.

One doesn't typically have to wonder what a toddler wants to do. They are more than willing to let you know everything they're thinking, positive or negative, and they can be painfully honest. But in our society, we are often cautioned to suppress certain feelings. Boys are told not to cry. We angrily tell our kids not to show anger. We find it off-putting when people show feelings of pride. We even call overly-happy people eccentric.

As a music teacher, I can tangibly see the extinguishing of joy from one grade to the next. When a group of kindergarteners is asked to sing, most of them will do so with wild abandon and glee. By the time kids reach middle-school choir, it is like pulling teeth to get any sort of expression out of them. They look like comatose zombies, and those who dare to be different by smiling or singing with emotion are called all kinds of names.

The same goes for healthy self-esteem. Ask a classroom of first graders which of them are good artists, and hands will shoot straight up. Ask the same question of a group of high schoolers, and even the good artists are likely to keep their hands down. With good intention, we train our future generations that it's not okay to give yourself a pat on the back for a job well done. Calling any sort of positive attention to yourself is typically seen as egotistical and wrong. I disagree with the notion that having a strong self-image automatically means one does not care about others. Good leaders must not only be attentive to the needs of those around them, they must also exhibit confidence and a feeling of self-worth.

It's not uncommon for us to tell others that their feelings are wrong. "You should not be worried." "You should not be depressed." "You shouldn't let that get to you." While we may mean well, we are only encouraging the person to crawl farther into a shell and feel abnormal. We can validate people's feelings and let them know they are heard even if we don't agree with them.

Sometimes we are afraid to voice our feelings for fear of ramifications, or we are afraid of looking foolish. It's best to voice our feelings in the moment rather than hold them in and regret it later. My mother once observed that she never heard her father tell her mother that he loved her, though her mother said it all the time. When my mother asked him about it, he said, "Some things are hard to say. I said it once." He also hadn't said it to his daughter, simply thanking her when she told him she loved him. Late in his life, he called my mother and awkwardly said he loved her. I wonder if he regretted not saying it before.

Sometimes we assume that other people know our feelings without our having to voice them. This can lead to miscommunication and resentment. It's best to share our feelings honestly and listen respectfully to the response. It's also important to read the other person's body language and facial expressions in order to have a full understanding. My brother's girlfriend cannot hear and therefore must rely on nonverbal cues to interpret meaning. She is uncanny at reading people's expressions and often asks me what's wrong before I even realize that I am displaying an upset demeanor. If only all of us could be so adept at reading one another.

Perhaps the most dire consequence of our tendency to keep our feelings in check is the lack of people who are willing to speak up when an injustice is occurring. We tend to rely on those few people who are brave enough to stick their neck out and demand the righting of wrongs. Change would happen much more readily if all of us joined our voices together toward a common cause. I hope one day we'll live in a world where it is unacceptable *not* to voice concern over matters that potentially harm our communities.

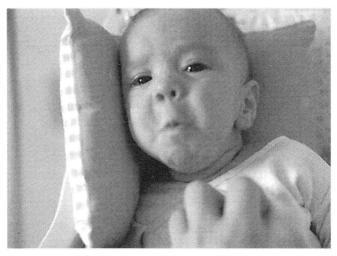
My son sharing some feelings

☑ Try This

☐ Use a journal to archive and honor the feelings you have in the course of a day.

☐ Let yourself have a good cry (or laugh) every now and then without feeling guilty.

☐ Send daily or weekly notes of gratitude to people who've helped you.

☐ Let people know when they've done something you admire.

☐ Write to friends whom you haven't contacted in a while and let them know why you're happy to have them in your life.

☐ Invite others to share their feelings. Avoid telling children their feelings are wrong.

☐ Say no to things you don't want to do.

SHOW YOUR FEELINGS

☐ Acknowledge your feelings about your current situation. Do some research on a job you've always dreamed of having. Could you change careers? Is there a place you'd rather be living?

☐ Look for the humor in everyday occurrences.

☐ Send back an order that isn't right without feeling guilty.

☐ Find ways you can express negative feelings while still considering the feelings of others.

☐ Try to reconcile some negative communication from the past by having an honest conversation about how you felt. Listen to the other person's side.

☐ Survey your family or employees in an effort to let their feelings be part of daily operations.

☐ Consider going to someone with whom you've held back your feelings and find a way to express yourself honestly.

☐ Speak up if you see a wrong-doing in progress.

☐ Choose a cause you support and join a rally or get a petition started.

☐ Think of a problem at your school or workplace and voice a solution for positive change.

☐ Think of something that is taking time away from things you'd rather do and gently release the responsibility.

☐ Make a playlist of songs that match different feelings and use it when you'd like to evoke or enhance a specific feeling.

Supplemental Materials

Hyperfocus List

Red things
Blue things
Black things
Yellow things
Green things
Orange things
Purple things
White things
Brown things
Tan things
Round things
Square things
Triangular things
Rectangular things
Oval things
Smooth things
Rough things
Soft things
Hard things
Metal things

Windows
Doors
Roofs
Chimneys
Bricks
Clouds
Leaves
Rocks
Trees
Water
Birds
Flowers
Animals
Shrubs
Bugs
Tail light shapes
Hubcaps
License plates
Power lines
Gates

SUPPLEMENTAL MATERIALS

Fabric things
Plastic things
Expensive things
Cheap things
Pretty things
Transparent things
Long things
Short things
Tiny things
Huge things
Dangerous things
Striped things
Polka-dotted things
Things inside of other things
Things on top of other things
Things that open and shut
Electronic things
Clothing items
Jewelry
Wall art
Décor
Curtains
Window shades
Liquid things
Edible things
Ears
Eyes
Hands
Mouths
Feet
Hair
The letter A (or other letters)
The number one (or other numbers)
Fences
Things far in the distance
Building facades
Lawn ornaments
Fire hydrants
Signs
Arrows
Curbs
Manhole covers
Things on the ground
Things in the sky
Logos
Driveways
Trash cans
Trash
Bicycles
Flags
Pedestrians
Traffic lights
Cracks
Porches
Airplanes
Pipes
Puddles
Acorns
Tattoos
Eyeglasses
Fingernails
Teeth
Shoes
Hats
Children
Elderly people

EYES OF WONDER

Add to the list here:

CREATIVE WRITING PROMPTS

Try answering with both
true and fabricated answers.

Describe your dream house.

Write about three things that happened today.

Describe yesterday from the viewpoint of your pet.

Write about a weird dream you remember having.

Describe the day your best friend is having today.

Write about a crush you had in school.

What's the sickest you've ever been?

Write about a time you got in trouble.

Write about your proudest moment.

Write about a ghost encounter you've had.

Write about your favorite trip.

Write about the last time you cried.

Write about something you think isn't fair.

Write about the most interesting job you ever had.

Write about how you met your spouse, partner, or best pal.

Write about an invention you'd like to see.

Write about what you think it will be like 20 years from now.

ACKNOWLEDGEMENTS

Thank you to my mom Carol Lindell, proofreader extraordinaire and world-class mother.

Thank you to my carefree Aunt Barbara for taking my brother Rusty and me on fun adventures in her blue Camaro.

Thank you to my Uncle Steff for maintaining his childlike spirit throughout his entire life.

Thank you to my husband Ethan for his unconditional love and support.

Thank you to Cheri Gillard for her sage authoring advice.

And especially, thank you to my son Chris Lucia for letting me see the world through his eyes.

ABOUT THE AUTHOR

Laurie Gabriel is a writer, public speaker, and musical performer. She graduated *summa cum laude* from the University of Denver and holds a Texas certificate in conflict resolution and mediation. Her teaching career spans over three decades. She has published resource guides for schools and is the producer of the documentary film *Heal Our Schools*. She has spoken across the USA about seeing the world through a child's lens. She delivered a Tedx Talk at Mountain View College in Dallas, Texas, and has presented numerous workshops at national education conferences. Laurie is an award-winning actress who performs regularly in musical theater productions. She has visited over fifty countries and is passionate about researching other cultures. Raising a child (who traveled to all those countries with her) has allowed her to see things from a more carefree perspective. She hopes she never loses the ability to see the world and its inhabitants through eyes of wonder. For more information visit LaurieGabriel.com.

Google Kumbayah Nappods

Belleview
Indiana
1877
Formerly Known as
Mud Flats

Beautiful view

Look around room

Beautiful view of the power of people

A magical moment takes place at a time in my life when

Before | After

current
imagination
creativity

disappointment

Made in the USA
Coppell, TX
12 January 2024